Malik and the Owl Cup

by Catherine Baker

illustrated by Beatriz Castro

Malik was in the garden.

“We must pull up the weeds,”
said Mum.

Weeding was so hard for Malik.
The weeds had long roots!

Malik dug with a trowel.

The soil got softer.

Now I can pull the weed up!

Malik hit an odd thing in the soil.

Look, Mum!
Dig it up.

The odd thing was dark red.

Malik took the cup to the tap.

Malik got all the soil off.
It was an owl cup!

"Can I have this cup, Mum?" said Malik.

Malik took the cup to his room.

The pens are in a mess.
I will put them in the cup!

"My owl cup is the best!" said Malik.

Encourage students to use the pictures to retell the story.